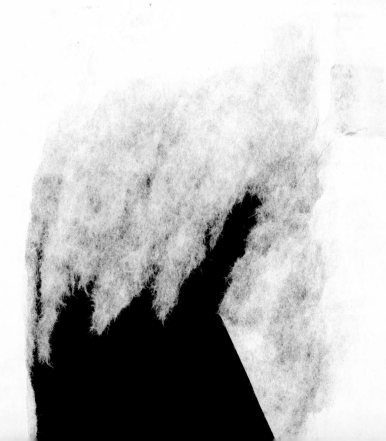

good answers
to tough questions

About Divorce

Written by Joy Berry

 CHILDRENS PRESS ®

CHICAGO

Managing Editor: Lana Eberhard
Copy Editors: Annette Gooch, Judy Lockwood
Contributing Editors: John Bilitch, Ph.D.,
Libby Byers, Ilene Frommer, James Gough, M.D.,
Dan Gurney, Charles Pengra, Ph.D.

Art Direction: Communication Graphics
Designer: Jennifer Wiezel
Illustration Designer: Bartholomew
Inking Artist: Nina Bonos
Lettering Artist: Linda Hanney
Coloring Artist: Christine McNamara
Typography and Production: Communication Graphics

Published by Childrens Press
in cooperation with Living Skills Press

This book can answer these questions about divorce:
- What is divorce?
- Why do people divorce?
- What happens to children after a divorce?
- How do children feel about divorce?
- How can children survive divorce?

Divorce legally ends a marriage between a husband and wife.

The legal reasons people get divorced are called **grounds for divorce**.

A *divorce decree* is a document containing all the details of the divorce. A divorce goes into effect and is said to be final when a judge signs the divorce decree.

In a **no-fault divorce** neither the husband or wife is held responsible for the failure of the marriage.

Grounds for a no-fault divorce include
- incompatibility or
- irreconcilable differences.

In a **fault divorce** either the husband or the wife holds the other person responsible for the failure of the marriage.

Grounds for a fault divorce include
- abandonment,
- adultery,
- cruelty,
- chemical addiction,
- fraud,
- imprisonment, or
- incurable mental illness.

Incompatibility is grounds for divorce. Incompatibility is the inability of a husband and wife to live together happily.

Irreconcilable differences are also grounds for divorce. Irreconcilable differences are disagreements about important issues between a husband and wife.

Abandonment is grounds for divorce. Abandonment happens when
- a husband leaves home permanently without getting permission from his wife, or
- a wife leaves home permanently without getting permission from her husband.

Adultery is grounds for divorce. Adultery happens when
- a husband has sexual relations with someone other than his wife, or
- a wife has sexual relations with someone other than her husband.

Cruelty is also grounds for divorce. Cruelty happens when
- a husband does something to mentally or physically harm his wife, or
- a wife does something to mentally or physically harm her husband.

Chemical addiction is grounds for divorce. Chemical addiction happens when a person becomes dependent on drugs or alcohol and cannot stop using them.

Fraud is also grounds for divorce. Fraud happens when
- a man lies to a woman in order to trick her into marrying him, or
- a woman lies to a man in order to trick him into marrying her.

Imprisonment is grounds for divorce. Imprisonment happens when a husband or wife is convicted of a crime and sent to prison for a long time.

Incurable mental illness is also grounds for divorce. Incurable mental illness happens when a person develops a mental disorder for which there is no known cure.

The divorce decree states how the children will be cared for after the parents separate.

Custody is the legal responsibility for taking care of a child until he or she becomes an adult.

Custodial parents are parents who have custody of their children.

Non-custodial parents are parents who do not have custody of their children.

Visitation rights entitle non-custodial parents to spend time with their children.

Child support is the money that non-custodial parents give to custodial parents to help pay for the things their children need.

In **sole custody,** *one* parent has custody of the child.

In some sole custody situations, the child lives with one parent and visits the other parent.

In other sole custody situations, the child lives with one parent and seldom, if ever, sees the other parent.

In *joint custody,* both parents share custody of the child.

There are several kinds of joint custody. In *joint legal custody,* the child lives with one parent but both parents have an equal part in making decisions that affect the child.

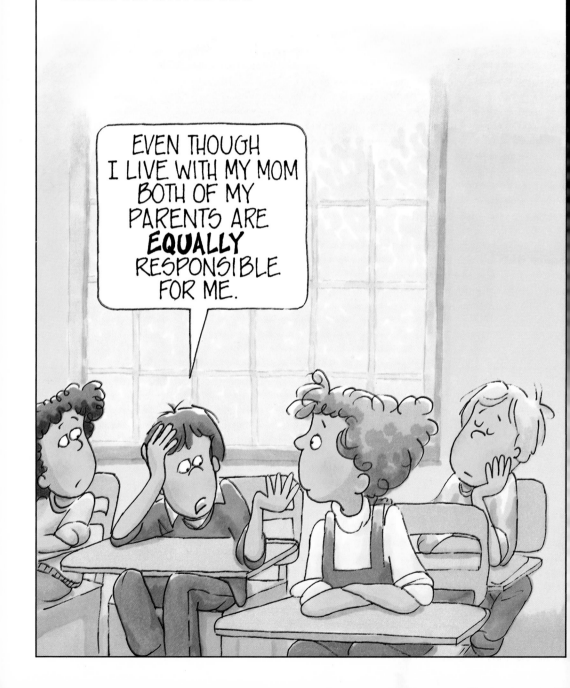

In *joint physical custody,* the child takes turns living with both parents but both parents continue to have an equal part in making decisions that affect the child.

In *joint alternating custody,* the child takes turns living with the parents and all of the decisions regarding the child are made by the parent the child is currently living with.

In joint physical or joint alternating custody, a child might
- spend several days a week with one parent and several days a week with the other parent,
- spend every other week with each parent,
- spend every other month with each parent,
- spend the time school is in session with one parent and school vacations with the other parent, or
- spend every other year with each parent.

In *third-party custody,* someone other than the parents has custody of the child. This situation can be either temporary or permanent. It occurs when neither parent chooses or is able to take care of the child. In third-party custody, the court chooses someone to take care of the child. The person is called the child's *guardian.* A relative of the child can be the child's guardian.

A person from a public agency or institution can also be a child's guardian.

The children of parents who divorce often feel
- *insecure* because they do not know what is going to happen to them as a result of their family's splitting up,
- *rejected* because at least one of their parents will be leaving them and moving into another home,
- *lonely* because at least one of their parents no longer lives with them,
- *guilty* because they feel they might have done something to cause the divorce, or
- *confused* because they do not know which parent to side with.

The children of parents who divorce might also feel
- *embarrassed* because they think that a family without two parents is inferior,
- *cheated* because things cannot be the way they want them to be,
- *powerless* because they feel they have no control over the situation,
- *angry* because their parents' divorce causes a great deal of pain and problems for the entire family, or
- *resentful* because the situation does not seem fair to the family members who did nothing to cause the divorce.

If your parents divorce, you can make things easier on yourself by following six steps.

STEP ONE — FACE IT.

Do not try to ignore what is happening. Admit that your parents are divorcing.

STEP TWO — ACCEPT IT.

Accept the fact that your parents' divorce is most likely final and that your father and mother will probably not get back together again.

STEP THREE — EXPLORE IT.

Find out the answers to these questions:
- Why did the divorce happen?
- When will the divorce go into effect? (When will it be final?)
- What is going to happen to you after the divorce?
  — Who will have custody of you?
  — Where will you live?
  — Who will be living with you?
  — When will you see your non-custodial parent?

It is best for everyone if you give both your parents an opportunity to answer your questions. You might want to have a long talk with your mother and another long talk with your father.

If your mother's answers to your questions are completely different from your father's answers, you might need to talk to an adult outside of your family. A good person to talk to is a professional family counselor provided by your parents or your school. This person can help you understand what is going on and why your parents are giving you different answers to your questions.

STEP FOUR — DEAL WITH YOUR EMOTIONS APPROPRIATELY.

It is important to acknowledge your feelings about the divorce, accept them, and then handle them appropriately.

If your parents' divorce causes you to feel **insecure,** do these things:

- Remember that as long as you are a child, there will be at least one adult to protect and take care of you.
- Realize that, in addition to your parents, there are other adults in your family or community who will help make sure that you have a family situation that is good for you.

If your parents' divorce causes you to feel **rejected,** do these things:

- Remember that your parents' divorce means that they are no longer married to one another. It does not mean that they are rejecting you.
- Realize that, no matter what happens, you will always be your parents' child and they will always love you.

If your parents' divorce causes you to feel **lonely**, do these things:

- Remember that it takes two people to create a relationship, and both people need to give to each other as well as receive from each other. Don't expect your parents to do all of the giving in your relationship with them. Think of things you can do to enhance your relationship with your parents and then do those things.
- Try not to expect the parent who does not live with you to make all of the effort to maintain a relationship with you. Do your best to keep in touch with this parent.
  — Call the parent on the telephone.
  — Write letters to the parent.
  — Help make plans for getting together with the parent.

If your parents' divorce causes you to feel **guilty,** do these things:
- Realize that you did not make your parents decide to divorce, so you cannot be blamed for their decision.
- Realize that parents divorce because of the problems they create for each other, not because of anything their children do. So, no matter how much you might have misbehaved, your misbehavior did not cause your parents' divorce.

If your parents' divorce causes you to feel **confused,** do these things:
- Remember that your parents' arguments are between them and should not involve you.
  - If possible, do not be around your parents while they are arguing with each other.
  - If you cannot be away from your parents while they are arguing, avoid becoming involved in the argument.
  - Avoid trying to decide which parent is right and which parent is wrong. Let them deal with their problems themselves.

- Remember that it is important for you to continue to love and have a relationship with both of your parents.
- Remember that you are not being disloyal to your mother by loving your father, and you are not being disloyal to your father by loving your mother. You have a right to love both of your parents, even though they no longer love each other.
  - Refuse to side with one parent against the other parent.
  - Try not to listen when one parent tells you bad things about the other parent.
  - Do not allow your parents to send messages to each other through you. Encourage them to talk directly to each other.

If your parents' divorce causes you to feel **embarrassed,** do these things:
- Remember that your situation is not unusual. There are many children whose parents are divorced.
- Realize that other people know that you have no control over your parents' relationship. No one will blame you or think less of you because your parents are divorced.

If your parents' divorce causes you to feel **_cheated,_** do these things:
- Remember that there is no such thing as a perfect situation. Try not to be disappointed because your situation is not perfect.
- Remember that there are good things about every situation. Try to find the good things about your situation. Then focus on the good rather than the bad things.
- Realize that children do not create family situations. Adults do. As a child, you might not be able to create the family situation that you would like to be a part of. However, when you are an adult, you can create a family situation that is acceptable to you. Think about the family situation you will create as an adult and look forward to the time when you will make it a reality.

If your parents' divorce causes you to feel **out of control,** do these things:
- Realize that even though you do not have control over what happens between your parents, you do have a certain amount of control over what happens between your parents and you. You cannot force your parents to get along with each other. However, by treating your parents kindly, you can make it easier for them to get along with you.
- Make sure that your parents know exactly how you feel and what you want in regard to
  — which parent you want to live with, and
  — when and where you want to see the parent who does not live with you.
- Talk to a caring adult if you are unable to share this information with your parents. Then ask the adult to talk with your parents.

I LIKE LIVING WITH MY MOTHER, BUT MORE OF THE TIME I'D LIKE TO LIVE WITH MY FATHER. I DON'T WANT TO TELL MY MOTHER THIS BECAUSE I DON'T WANT TO HURT HER FEELINGS.

If your parents' divorce causes you to feel **_angry,_** do these things:
- Avoid taking your anger out on people who have nothing to do with the divorce.
- Talk about your anger with your parents or with other adults who can help you deal with the divorce.
- You might want to express your anger by crying, yelling, jumping up and down, or hitting things. It is OK to do these things as long as you do not bother other people or damage or destroy anything. This might mean that you will need to go outside or into another room while you express your anger.

If your parents divorce causes you to feel **resentful,** do these things:
- Realize that feeling resentful can cause you to be extremely unhappy. It can also cause you to become physically ill. Thus, it is important for you to try to overcome feeling resentful. It will help if you remember that
  — a bad marriage creates a lot of bad feelings and problems for everyone;
  — no one (including your parents) should have to stay in a bad marriage for any reason; and
  — in the end, doing away with a bad marriage that cannot be repaired is the best thing for the children as well as their parents.

- Try to forgive your parents. Forgiving your parents can help you let go of the resentment you feel toward them. Your forgiveness can help your parents handle any guilt they might feel over how their divorce has affected you. Because resentment and guilt make people unhappy and can cause them to become physically ill, it will be good for you to forgive your parents and for your parents to feel forgiven. It will help to remember that
  — no one is perfect, everyone makes mistakes (this is true of your parents and it is true of you); and
  — if you are willing to forgive your parents when they make a mistake, they will most likely be more willing to forgive you when you make a mistake.

STEP FIVE —
DO YOUR BEST TO ADJUST TO YOUR NEW SITUATION.

Make a list of the things you did not like about living with your parents when they were still married. (The tension that existed between your parents and the arguments they had with each other will most likely be on your list.) Anytime you begin to wish that things were the way they used to be,
- look at the list and
- be thankful that you do not have to deal with the things on the list anymore.

Make a list of everything you like about your new situation. Add to this list every time you discover another thing you like. Anytime you begin to feel bad about your situation,
- look at your list and
- be thankful for the good things about your new situation.

Work with your parents to make your new situation good for everyone it affects by doing these things:

- Find out exactly what your parents' divorce decree says about child custody. Once you know about the custody arrangements, abide by them as best as you can.
- Try not to take advantage of your parents at this time. When you are with them,
  — do not demand to be entertained,
  — do not demand that they buy you things, and
  — do not make your parents feel that they must compete with each other for your love and approval.

STEP SIX — TALK ABOUT YOUR THOUGHTS AND FEELINGS.

It is important to continue talking about your thoughts and feelings until your parents' divorce no longer disturbs you.

- Keeping a diary or journal can help you get in touch with and express your thoughts and feelings.
- Talking to people who have already gone through what you are experiencing can be comforting and reassuring. It can also give you valuable information about what you can do to help yourself survive the divorce.

Don't think that talking once or twice about your parents' divorce will make you feel better immediately. It might take you as long as one or two years to have all of your questions answered and to adjust to your new situation.

In most cases, both the mother and the father stay in touch with their child after a divorce. However in a few situations, this is not true. If you have a parent who, despite all of your efforts to keep in touch, does not stay in touch with you, you need to do these things:

- Remember that it is not normal for parents not to stay in touch with their children.
- Do not think that there is something wrong with you.
- Realize that there is probably something wrong with your parent. Parents who do not make an effort to stay in touch with their children have problems and might need professional help.

I KEPT TRYING TO KEEP IN TOUCH WITH MY DAD, BUT HE WOULD NEVER ANSWER MY LETTERS OR PHONE CALLS. AT FIRST I THOUGHT MAYBE SOMETHING WAS WRONG WITH ME. BUT THEN I BEGAN TO REALIZE THAT **HE** WAS THE ONE WITH THE PROBLEMS, NOT ME!

You have a right to be happy and so do your parents. Allow your parents to live their new life as they choose. It will help if you remember that in a few years you will be an adult and you will be able to live your life the way you choose to live it.

Although divorce may seem to be a negative thing to happen to a family, it can have a positive effect on family members if everyone works together to turn it into something positive.